DRAGONFLIES

by Patrick Merrick

Content Adviser:
Jeffrey Hahn,
Department of Entomology,
University of Minnesota

Published in the United States of America by The Child's World®
PO Box 326 • Chanhassen, MN 55317-0326
800-599-READ • www.childsworld.com

PHOTO CREDITS
© Adam Jones/Dembinsky Photo Associates: 11
© Buddy Mays/Getty Images: 6–7
© E. R. Degginger/Dembinsky Photo Associates: 5, 16–17, 23
© Gary Meszaros/Dembinsky Photo Associates: 12–13, 19, 25, 26–27
© Gary Meszaros/Photo Researchers, Inc.: 20–21
© Mark Cassino/Dembinsky Photo Associates: 8, 14–15
© Skip Moody/Dembinsky Photo Associates: cover, 28

ACKNOWLEDGMENTS
The Child's World®: Mary Berendes, Publishing Director;
Katherine Stevenson, Editor

The Design Lab: Kathleen Petelinsek, Design and Page Production

LIBRARY OF CONGRESS CATALOGING-IN-PUBLICATION DATA
Merrick, Patrick.
 Dragonflies / by Patrick Merrick.
   p. cm. — (New naturebooks)
 Includes bibliographical references and index.
 ISBN 1-59296-635-7 (library bound : alk. paper)
 1. Dragonflies—Juvenile literature. I. Title. II. Series.
 QL520.M37 2006
 595.7'33—dc22   2006001363

Table of Contents

On the cover: This green darner dragonfly is resting on a sumac leaf. Its wings are still wet with dew in the cool morning air.

Meet the Dragonfly!

There are about 5,000 different kinds of dragonflies.

If you sit quietly by a pond on a warm summer day, you might see many different things. Perhaps a fish will jump in the water. A fuzzy raccoon might hurry across the beach. And you'll probably see flies and mosquitoes buzzing around in the air.

Soon you might see a colorful creature zooming around with the other bugs. If you watch long enough, you'll see it catch and eat the other bugs. What kind of creature can catch these flying bugs so quickly? It's a dragonfly!

This green darner dragonfly is zooming after bugs on a warm sunny day.

What Do Dragonflies Look Like?

Dragonflies aren't flies at all. Flies have one pair of wings, while dragonflies have two.

Dragonflies are a kind of **insect**. An insect is an animal with three separate parts to its body. It has a head, a middle section (called a *thorax*), and a tail end (called an *abdomen*). Like most insects, dragonflies have wings and six legs. Some insects have only one pair of wings, but dragonflies, like most insects, have two pairs.

This darner dragonfly is resting on a branch in Arkansas. There are many different kinds of darners. Green darners are one of the most common.

Dragonflies have been around for a very long time. In fact, they have been around longer than any other living insects. The earliest dragonflies lived about 300 million years ago. They were the largest insects of all time. They had a **wingspan** of over 24 inches (61 cm)! That's bigger than the wingspan of most birds.

Many people confuse dragonflies with damselflies. You can tell them apart by looking at their eyes and their wings. Dragonflies have huge eyes that are close together, while damselflies' eyes are much farther apart. When dragonflies rest, they hold their wings straight out from their bodies. Damselflies hold their wings close to their abdomens.

This ruby meadowhawk is resting on a flower. There are many different kinds of meadowhawks, and they live all across the United States.

How Do Dragonflies See?

A dragonfly's eyes are so large, they often touch each other.

The adult dragonfly is made for flying. Its long, thin body and long wings move through the air quickly. To help it see, the dragonfly has a round head that can turn almost all the way around! If you look closely, you'll see that the dragonfly has huge eyes. These eyes help the hungry dragonfly see its next meal.

The outside of your eye has a curved, clear cover called a **lens**. The lens helps you see clearly, like the lenses in a pair of glasses. But a dragonfly's eye has 30,000 different lenses! These lenses let the dragonfly look in all directions at once. It can see other bugs moving from very far away.

From close up, you can really see the detail of this dragonfly's eyes. Look at just one of the eyes. Each one of the small dots is a lens!

What Do Dragonflies' Wings Look Like?

Most insects fold their wings over their backs when they rest. But dragonflies can't fold their wings—they must rest with their wings held straight out from their bodies.

Dragonflies have amazing wings. Most dragonflies have wingspans of two to three inches (5 to 8 cm). Dragonflies that live in warm jungle areas can have wingspans of up to 8 inches (20 cm)— that's about as long as your foot! A dragonfly's wings are made of thin, clear skin. You can see right through them! The clear skin is criss-crossed with hollow tubes called **veins**. The veins carry blood through the wings. Some dragonflies' wings also have blue, black, or brown patches.

You can clearly see the veins in the wings of this riffle snaketail dragonfly. Riffle snaketails have a wingspan of about two inches (5 cm).

12

Dragonflies not only have two pairs of wings, they can move each pair separately. These strong wings let the dragonflies float in the air or zip quickly in any direction—even backwards! Some dragonflies can fly faster than 30 miles (48 km) an hour.

Dragonflies' wings aren't the same size. Their front wings are smaller than their back wings.

Here you can see a 12-spotted skimmer as it rests on a twig in Michigan. Try counting the spots on its wings. How do you think these dragonflies got their name?

Are Dragonflies Helpful?

Dragonflies got their name because of their jaws, which looked like a dragon's jaws to some people.

At one time dragonflies were called "horse stingers," "snake doctors," "snake feeders," and even "Devil's darning needles." People were afraid of dragonflies and gave them scary names. They had no reason to be afraid. Dragonflies don't hurt people. In fact, they're a big help! They eat insect pests such as flies and mosquitoes.

Painted skimmers like this one are often confused with Halloween pennant dragonflies. Both insects are black and orange, but painted skimmers have spots on their wings, while Halloween pennants have bands.

What Are Dragonfly Babies Like?

Some types of dragonfly eggs hatch in as little as five days.

Adult dragonflies live for about one year. During this time, the male and female dragonflies mate. The female lays her eggs underwater, in a pond or stream. A large female dragonfly can lay up to a thousand eggs in a clump. She needs to lay a lot of eggs because fish and other insects will eat many of them.

After about a month, the eggs hatch. The new babies don't look anything like dragonflies. They don't even have wings. They look like little swimming worms. These baby dragonflies are called **naiads**. A naiad is a kind of **larva**, which is a general word for a baby insect. Naiads are insect larvae that live in the water.

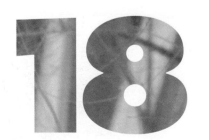

This green darner dragonfly naiad is waiting for its next meal to swim by. You can see that the naiad looks nothing like the adult on page 7.

Dragonfly naiads are made for living underwater. Their dirty green or brownish color lets them hide. They look like the mud and weeds at the bottom of the pond or stream. They can even change color to match the objects around them. This ability to hide against their background is called **camouflage**.

A naiad wants to do only one thing—eat. Under its mouth, the naiad has one or two large spikes at the end of a long lip. When the naiad sees something good to eat, it reaches out and spears the food with its lip spikes. Then it brings the food back to its mouth to eat.

Some kinds of naiads hunt for their food, while others simply wait for their next meal to swim by.

This darner dragonfly naiad has caught a small fish in an Ohio pond.

21

Do Baby Dragonflies Have Enemies?

Naiads also stay safe by keeping very still for long periods of time.

While waiting for food, dragonfly naiads are in danger of being eaten. Fish, birds, and other insects love to eat the naiads. Animals that eat other animals are called **predators**. To survive, the naiads must learn to escape from predators. If they are in danger, they swim away quickly. Naiads can move extra fast by using a trick—they suck water into their rear ends, and then squirt it back out. This pushes the naiad quickly through the water—and away from danger.

This dragonfly naiad is clinging to a blade of underwater grass. It thought the photographer might be an enemy, so it stayed still for a long time after this picture was taken.

What Is Molting?

It takes about two hours for a dragonfly to molt. It takes about two days for the newly molted dragonfly's colors to develop.

Baby dragonflies live as wormlike naiads for about three years. During that time they keep eating and growing. They don't grow like people do, because their skin is too hard and shell-like. When a naiad gets too big for its skin, it sheds the skin, or **molts**. Underneath there is a new, bigger skin. A naiad molts up to 10 times before it becomes an adult dragonfly.

When the naiad is ready to molt for the last time, it crawls onto a stick hanging over the water. There the naiad molts into an adult dragonfly. This is a dangerous time for the young insect. It must sit in the sun to harden its body and wings. Until those parts harden, it cannot fly. While it is waiting, it is in danger of being eaten by passing birds or hungry fish.

This eastern pond hawk has just molted for the last time. You can see how much smaller the old skin (on the right) was. The dragonfly now waits patiently as its new wings and skin harden.

What Do Dragonflies Eat?

Dragonflies beat their wings about 35 times each second.

Dragonflies feed in two ways. *Hawking* **is flying after prey and catching it in midair.** *Sallying* **is sitting in one spot, darting out to catch prey, and then returning to the same spot to eat.**

Once a dragonfly can fly, it spends most of its time in the air. It flies around all day looking for food. Dragonflies are always hungry. Sometimes they drop to the surface of a pond and scoop up a little fish or frog. Often, though, they eat smaller flying insects. They catch them right out of the air! When a dragonfly sees an insect flying, it charges toward it. Then it folds its front legs together to form a basket. The dragonfly uses this basket to catch the insect in midair.

This dragonhunter is eating a 12-spotted skimmer. Dragonhunters feed on butterflies and other dragonflies— some almost as big as the dragonhunters themselves.

Today dragonflies live in almost every country. You can usually find them near ponds, lakes, or rivers. They have even been found in deserts and mountains. So, the next time you are sitting in the summer sun, keep your eye out for the dragonfly. It is truly one of the most interesting creatures on Earth!

Some kinds of dragonflies can fly for great distances. Wandering gliders have been spotted over the ocean, hundreds of miles from land!

This spangled skimmer is resting on a lily in Michigan.

Glossary

camouflage (KAM-uh-flazh) Camouflage is coloring that lets animals blend in with whatever is around them. Dragonfly naiads use camouflage to hide from enemies.

insect (IN-sekt) Insects are animals that have six legs, wings, a hard outer shell, and bodies divided into three main parts. Dragonflies are insects.

larva (LAR-vuh) A larva is a young insect. Dragonfly larvae (LAR-vee) are also called naiads.

lens (LENZ) The lens is the curved, clear surface of your eye that keeps things from looking fuzzy. Dragonflies have 30,000 lenses in each eye.

molt (MOLT) When an insect molts, it sheds its outer layer of skin to uncover a new skin underneath. Dragonflies molt up to 15 times as they grow.

naiad (NY-ad) A naiad is a young dragonfly. Dragonfly naiads live underwater and have no wings.

predators (PREH-duh-turz) Predators are animals that hunt other animals for food. Dragonflies are predators.

prey (PRAY) Prey are animals that other animals hunt as food. Other insects are common prey for dragonflies.

veins (VAYNZ) Veins are hollow tubes that move blood around. Dragonflies have veins in their clear wings.

wingspan (WING-span) The wingspan of a bird or insect is the distance between the ends of its wings when the wings are spread out. Long ago, dragonflies had wingspans of two feet.

To Find Out More

Read It!

Allen, Judy, and Tudor Humphries (illustrator). *Are You a Dragonfly?* New York: Kingfisher, 2001.

Bernhard, Emery, and Durga Bernhard (illustrator). *Dragonfly.* New York: Holiday House, 1993.

Pascoe, Elaine, and Dwight Kuhn (photographer). *Dragonflies and Damselflies.* New York: Blackbirch Press, 2005.

Rinehart, Susie Caldwell, and Anisa Claire Hovemann (illustrator). *Eliza and the Dragonfly.* Nevada City, CA: Dawn Publications, 2004.

On the Web

Visit our home page for lots of links about dragonflies: *http://www.childsworld.com/links*

Note to Parents, Teachers, and Librarians: We routinely check our Web links to make sure they're safe, active sites—so encourage your readers to check them out!

31

Index

About the Author

When Pat Merrick was a child, his family traveled and moved many times. He became fascinated with science and finding out about the world around him. In college he majored in science and education. After, college, Mr. Merrick and his wife both decided to become teachers and try and help kids learn to love the world around them. He has taught science to all levels of kids from kindergarten through twelfth grade. When not teaching or writing, Mr. Merrick loves to read and play with his six children. He currently lives in a small town in southern Minnesota with his wife and family.